THE GIANT PANDA

Hope for Tomorrow

Carol A. Amato
Illustrated by David Wenzel

BARRON'S

Acknowledgment
Many thanks to Heather Angel for her help and guidance in the preparation of this book. Heather Angel is a wildlife photographer and author of the outstanding book, *Pandas* (Voyageur Press, 1998), which is highly recommended for further reading.

Dedication
To Aunt Ella, who believed so fervently in these little books and gave to me her unconditional love and support.

Metric Equivalents
Page 9:
5 to 6 feet (150 to 280 centimeters)
165 to 250 pounds (70 to 113 kilograms)
Page 12:
22 to 40 pounds (10 to 18 kilograms)
Page 35:
4 ounces (112 grams)
Page 43:
10 to 12 feet (3 to 3.5 meters)
12 pounds (5.40 kilograms)

Text © Copyright 2000 by Carol A. Amato
Illustrations © Copyright 2000 by Barron's Educational Series, Inc.

All inquiries should be addressed to:
Barron's Educational Series, Inc.
250 Wireless Boulevard
Hauppauge, New York 11788
http://www.barronseduc.com

International Standard Book No. 0-7641-1334-8

Library of Congress Catalog Card No. 00-035440

Library of Congress Cataloging-in-Publication Data

Amato, Carol A.
    The giant panda : the hope for tomorrow / Carol A. Amato ; illustrated by David Wenzel.
        p. cm.—(Young readers' series)
    Includes bibliographical references (p. 46)
    ISBN 0-7641-1334-8
    1. Giant panda—Juvenile literature. [1. Giant panda. 2. Pandas. 3. Endangered species.] I. Wenzel, David, 1950–, ill. II. Title.
    QL737.C214 A42   2000
    599.789—dc21   00-035440

PRINTED IN HONG KONG
9 8 7 6 5 4 3 2 1

Table of Contents

"Honk, honk . . . honk, honk."

It was early morning. Ming Chi sat up in her bed and listened.

"Huff, huff, huff, huff."

Ming Chi had never heard sounds like this before. She looked out of her window. The blizzard of the day before surrounded the Panda Research and Rescue Center with deep snow, and it was still falling.

"Oh, my," she said. Curled up against the corner of one of the buildings was a giant panda. Its calls meant it was quite upset. Ming Chi ran to tell her father.

This excitement was very new to Ming Chi, who had just arrived at the Center a few days before to visit her scientist father. The Center is in a large reserve in China where pandas are protected. He was working there for one year to study ways to help these endangered animals.

Ming Chi ran into her father's room.

"*Jo sahn* (jo-san), *Bàba*" ("Good morning, Father"), Ming Chi said excitedly.

"It is very early, Ming Chi, so . . ."

"But, *Bàba*, there is a panda outside, near my bedroom window!"

Her father began to dress quickly. Ming Chi ran back to her room to dress also. Soon they were outside with the workers.

"Stay back here," warned her father. He walked closer to the panda. It was trembling and covered its eyes when he came near.

"The panda may be sick," he said to the workers. "We must examine it."

One of the workers used a long jab stick to tranquilize the panda. In ten minutes, it was in a deep sleep. They carried it into the exam room on a stretcher.

Ming Chi was speechless. She watched as her father examined the panda.

Soon he exclaimed to the workers, "This is Ping-Ping! See the black patch on her face?"

They all agreed.

"She lost her radio collar, Ming Chi," he explained. "We have been tracking her for a long time. We named her Ping-Ping, which means 'peaceful.'"

"Why does she have a radio, *Bàba*?" asked Ming Chi, looking quite surprised.

"This is a special radio, Ming Chi," explained her father. "Researchers capture pandas in harmless traps and fit them with radio collars so they can find out about their location and whether they are active or resting. The collar sends beeping signals to the researchers."

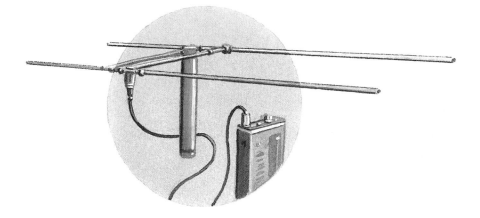

"When we followed Ping-Ping seven months ago, we discovered she had a cub," said her father.

"Where is the cub now?" asked Ming Chi.

"That is something to worry about," he answered. "Sometimes giant pandas come down from the mountains during a blizzard or when they are sick or starving. They may even seek out people for help. Because panda mothers take good care of their babies, Ping-Ping may have known she was too sick to care for it."

"*Bàba*, why is it called a *giant* panda? It doesn't look very big to me."

"It is called a giant panda because there is another panda in China called the red panda, which is much smaller," he answered. "Giant pandas are about 5 to 6 feet standing up and weigh from 165 to 250 pounds. Some males can even be larger."

"May I touch her?" asked Ming Chi.

Her father nodded his head.

"Her fur looks soft, but it's so rough and stiff," she said.

"Yes," Father said. "Her thick, oily fur is good protection in the damp, misty habitat of China's mountains."

"What will happen to Ping-Ping now?" asked Ming Chi.

"I think she has a stomach infection. We will give her medicine, a special diet of rice porridge, and plenty of bamboo. If she becomes strong enough, we will release her. Our job is to help as many pandas as we can now and to find ways to protect them in the future."

The workers gently placed Ping-Ping in a holding pen. The pen opened into a large enclosure that looked like the panda's natural habitat. The researchers can observe Ping-Ping and other pandas there. They left sugar water for quick energy, the porridge, and plenty of bamboo for her.

"*Bàba*, I thought pandas only ate bamboo," said Ming Chi. "She would not find rice porridge in the mountains."

Her father laughed. "You are right, Ming Chi. They do not eat this kind of food in the wild. Their diet is mostly bamboo . . . lots and lots of bamboo. In fact, pandas eat about 22 to 40 pounds of bamboo every day. They eat for about eight hours and then sleep for one to four hours, right around the clock. Even at night, they can find the best bamboo by using their sense of smell."

"Don't pandas eat anything else besides bamboo?" asked Ming Chi.

"Now and then they will eat wildflowers, fruits, and even dead animals if they find them," answered Father. "In captivity, they are able to eat other foods as well."

"Then why don't they in the wild?" asked Ming Chi.

"Well, daughter," began her father, "there is some history to your question! A few million years ago, the ancestors of the giant panda were meat-eaters, or carnivores. When they could not find much prey, they began eating bamboo, which was everywhere. After many, many years of eating just bamboo, the pandas couldn't change their eating habits. With the stomach of a carnivore, they still can't digest bamboo well and must eat a lot of it to survive."

"But, *Bàba*, can the pandas find enough bamboo to eat?" asked Ming Chi.

"Long ago they could, but often now they cannot," answered her father. "China has so many people. More and more of the forests are used to build houses and much of the land is cleared for farming. Hunters, called poachers, kill the pandas for their fur coats, which they sell for lots of money. Anyone now caught doing this faces the death penalty. It is not easy for pandas to survive.

"There's another big problem, too," continued her father. "About every fifty years, the bamboo flowers, sets its seeds, and then dies. When this die-back happens over a big area, the panda must search for bamboo that is not flowering. When humans are on all sides, pandas have nowhere to go in their search. Pandas must leave their home ranges and go higher and higher into the mountains to try to find safety and bamboo."

"So now what will become of Ping-Ping and the other pandas?" Ming Chi asked.

"We cannot be sure," her father answered. "For now, there are many people trying to save them and their bamboo habitat."

"I will help, too," said Ming Chi.

"Good," he replied. "You can begin by watching Ping-Ping for a while to let us know how she behaves."

He and the workers left.

"Please eat and get strong," Ming Chi said to Ping-Ping.

Soon Ping-Ping woke up. She huffed and snorted. Those panda sounds meant that *she* was worried, too.

Ming Chi stayed with the panda all day, going inside only to eat and warm up.

Just before dark, her father called, "Come in, Ming Chi. You must go to sleep early if you want to come with us to search for Ping-Ping's cub."

This was a surprise for Ming Chi. That night she was so excited, she could barely sleep.

Chapter 3   One Cub Alone

The next morning, high in the mountains far above the reserve, strong winds still blew. The snow had stopped falling and hung heavily on the tall fir trees. Clouds drifted through the trees. Many miles down from the highest peaks, a young panda peeked his head out of a cave. He stepped carefully into the snow and looked around. Then he rolled around in the snow and playfully tumbled down a small hill, crashing into high stalks of bamboo. The cub now looked more like a little polar bear than a panda! He shook the snow from his fur and looked around. His mother was nowhere to be seen. She left him to find food three days ago. Mother pandas often leave their young for up to two days.

The cub wants his mother's milk, because he will nurse until he's about a year old. At six months old, he is just learning how to eat bamboo by copying his mother. He learns how to grasp a bamboo stalk with his front paws. His thumb, which is really part of his wristbone, will help him to peel away the tough outer layers of the stalk. For now, he prefers to eat the more tender leaves.

At about a year old, he will begin to search for food with his mother. When he's an adult, his strong jaw will be able to crush even the thickest bamboo stalks.

As the cub was about to eat some leaves, a huge leopard leaped down from a boulder a few feet away from him. The little panda scrambled up a spruce tree just as the big cat pounced at him! Trembling, he sat in the fork of the spruce, looking down at the leopard who was looking up and smacking its lips. The cat paced around the tree for several minutes, but did not climb the tree. It crouched down to wait. Sooner or later, the cub must come down.

"Be careful on the bridge. Wait for us," Ming Chi's father shouted to her.

Ming Chi waited for her father and the workers to catch up to her. They had been walking a long time and, so far, there were no signs of pandas.

"Do you think we will find a panda?" asked Ming Chi.

22

"There's always hope," her father answered. "Because pandas now live only in three provinces in central China, we will need to be lucky to see one. There are only about one thousand left in the wild, which means the giant panda is one of the most endangered animals in the world."

"But, *Bàba*, how will we know if pandas live around here?" asked Ming Chi.

"First, we can look for signs that the panda has left behind," he replied. "Look for tracks in the snow or their droppings, called spoor. The spoor can tell us when the panda was here and what it ate."

"I didn't know droppings could talk!" said Ming Chi.

Everyone laughed at Ming Chi's joke.

"There are many signs we can discover *without* words, Ming Chi," said her father. "Look over here. There are some broken-off bamboo stalks where the panda stopped to eat and a pressed-down spot where it rested. Pandas also leave messages for other pandas by marking rocks, trees, and other things with a scent from a special gland. This message may say, "Here I am," or "There I was!"

"Wow!" exclaimed Ming Chi. "It's like being a detective. A panda detective!"

The group continued to walk up the mountain, resting often. They stopped to eat under a tall fir tree. It was very quiet as the wind whistled through the openings between the mountains. Ming Chi broke the silence.

"*Bàba*, why doesn't the giant panda hibernate like other bears?"

"Well," he answered, "I will have to do some explaining before I can answer your question."

"For a long time, scientists argued about whether the panda belonged in the bear or the raccoon family. You see, the giant panda has many things in common with both animals. Most scientists now believe the panda is a bear but . . . a bear that doesn't hibernate! It can't build up enough body fat to last all winter. The panda can take care of itself during the long, hard winters and so . . ."

"Excuse me, *Bàba*," interrupted Ming Chi, "but I hear a dog barking."

"Shhh," said Li Feng, one of the researchers. "That barking is the sound a panda makes when it is excited or senses danger."

They all looked around.

"Over there," whispered Li Feng, pointing to a bamboo thicket.

"*Bei-shung*! *Bei-shung*!" ("Panda! Panda!") someone said excitedly.

There, indeed, was a large panda hidden in the bamboo. It could hardly be seen because its black markings blended in with the shadows.

"Oh, my," exclaimed Ming Chi's father. "It's Shi-Shi. She is far away from her home range."

"*Baaa, baaa!*" bleated Shi-Shi.

"She sounds like a goat," said Ming Chi.

"That's a friendly sound," explained her father. "Shi-Shi is very gentle. Pandas are different from one another, just as people differ. They can't talk, so they make sounds and show how they feel in other ways."

Ming Chi stepped closer to Shi-Shi.

"No, Ming Chi," warned her father. "Although this panda is usually gentle, like all wild animals, we cannot know what she may do next. Pandas may all look tame and cuddly, but they can be dangerous."

Shi-Shi rolled on her back as an invitation to play. Everyone laughed. In the next minute, she curled up and fell off to sleep. Like other pandas, she slept easily and stayed by herself most of the time.

"*Zai jian* (dsai-jee-an) . . . Good-bye, Shi-Shi," said Ming Chi as they left her to rest peacefully.

The group had not gone far when Ming Chi said,
"Now, what is *that*? It sounds like a pig!"
They all heard a loud squeal.
"It sounds like it's coming from over there," said Li Feng

Before they could change direction, something ran by
them, but it was hidden in the dense underbrush. They
followed the squealing sounds, which were now louder
than ever!

In the tall spruce tree ahead of them was the panda cub.

"So *that's* who was causing all the noise!" exclaimed
Ming Chi's father, pointing to the tree.

"By the looks of those tracks, a leopard was hoping to
have a little panda for lunch!"

Ming Chi looked up at the cub with wonder.

"The little one looks very afraid," said Li Feng. "I don't
think it will come down without some help."

Li Feng climbed up the tree slowly, so he would not frighten the cub. When he got within arm's reach, the baby panda swatted at him with his forepaws and made a screaming bark.

"Tough little one," Li Feng called down, laughing. He took off his jacket and quickly wrapped it around the cub. Still, by the time they got the young panda into the transport cage, Li Feng had many scratches.

"Say hello to Ping-Ping's baby, Ming Chi," said Li Feng. "It's a boy, and a brave little fellow at that."

"Hello, brave little one," Ming Chi whispered, still amazed by what had happened. The cub, quickly forgetting his anger, had nodded off to sleep.

They headed back down the mountain.

"How do you know it's Ping-Ping's cub?" asked Ming Chi.

"Ping-Ping is the only panda who's given birth in this area," answered Li Feng.

"We found Ping-Ping when her baby was born in the early fall. A mother panda usually has only one cub, but sometimes she has two. It is hard for her to take care of two cubs."

"Where is the cub's father?" asked Ming Chi.

"The male panda leaves right after mating with the female," answered Li Feng. "This isn't mean, but just the way bears and many other animal fathers behave. Some animal fathers, like wolves, help to care for their young."

"How can the mother take care of her baby all by herself?" asked Ming Chi.

"Like many other animal mothers who care for their babies alone, the mother panda knows how to take very good care of her cub. She usually doesn't

feed for twenty-five days after it's born and even eats
the baby's wastes, because the smell could attract
predators," said Li Feng.

"That's some good mother!" exclaimed Ming Chi.

"She has to be," said Li Feng. "When the cub is born,
it is so small, it can fit into the palm of your hand. It's
less than 4 ounces! It's pink with fine white fur and
doesn't look like a bear at all. The mother must be
very careful not to crush the baby, and she carries it
everywhere. The cub will not leave her arms during
the first twenty-six or so days. She also carries the
cub in her mouth."

"We'd better walk more quickly," said Ming Chi's
father. "We must get back before dark."

Tired and hungry, they reached the Panda Center as the sun was setting.

"I'm so hungry, I could eat a bear!" said Ming Chi.

"We hope it won't be a *panda* bear." Li Feng laughed.

"First we have to take care of the little one," said Ming Chi's father.

They brought the cub inside to examine him. He was quiet now and did not seem afraid when Ming Chi's father examined his ears and his eyes.

"Pandas have such little eyes, *Bàba*," said Ming Chi.

"Yes," he said. "The big black patches around their eyes make them look larger than they really are. This may help to frighten predators."

"How else are pandas protected?" asked Ming Chi.

"Their senses of smell and hearing are the most helpful to them. The adults have few predators. Because of these things, they can live about twenty years in the wild if they can find enough food and habitat."

Ming Chi's father tried to feel the cub's belly, but the cub pushed him away.

"You *are* a strong one," he said, "and healthy, too."

"If I could name him, I'd call him 'Yong-Yong,' because it means brave and strong," said Ming Chi.

"Then Yong-Yong it is!" her father said. "And now for the big moment."

Yong-Yong was put into the transport cage again and brought outside to Ping-Ping's holding pen. Li Feng placed the cage inside.

"We will see how Ping-Ping reacts before we open the door," he said.

As soon as Yong-Yong saw Ping-Ping, he began squealing. Ping-Ping walked cautiously toward the box and sniffed the cub. Then she bleated softly. Li Feng reached in and opened the door of the box. Yong-Yong ran to his mother, who greeted him with a loud, "*YIP, YIP, YIP!*" The cub quickly began nursing.

Everyone clapped their hands and cheered.

"Before long we will set them free," said Ming Chi's father. "Ping-Ping seems to be doing well, and in a few weeks she will be strong enough to take care of her cub in the wild."

"How long will Yong-Yong stay with Ping-Ping?" asked Ming Chi.

"Until he is eighteen to twenty-two months old, if they both survive," answered her father.

"What do you mean, *Bàba*? I thought you said that Ping-Ping was just fine."

"She is, Ming Chi," he said, "but like other giant pandas, she and Yong-Yong will have many threats to their survival. We will hope that the Chinese government and the environmental groups who help them will be able to save this special creature."

Ming Chi watched Ping-Ping as she held her cub lovingly in her arms.

"I hope so, *Bàba*. In my heart I wish for them and for all the pandas . . . *jiabei* (j-ya-bay) *xi wang* (shi-wang) . . . double hope—hope for today and hope for tomorrow!"

Afterword

The giant panda has been around for about 3 million years. It has been mentioned in Chinese books for over 2,000 years and was known as *da xiong mao* (da-shung-mao), which means large bear-cat. The panda is a symbol for China as the bald eagle is for the United States. Today, however, it is one of the world's rarest animals. In the past, many countries received pandas as gifts from the Chinese government. In a few zoos in the United States, scientists sometimes attempt to breed pandas. A panda cub (named Hua Mei) was born in August 1999 at the San Diego (California) Zoo. This birth will enable scientists to observe infant and mother behavior.

In November 1999, China loaned ZooAtlanta (Georgia) two pandas (Yang-Yang and Lun-Lun) for ten years. The zoo is raising money to fund their giant panda research project. Research in China is being conducted on captive pandas at the Chengdu Zoo and the Chengdu Research Base of Giant Panda Breeding.

Some scientists hope that captive-bred pandas can someday be released into the wild. Other scientists feel it is more important to focus on habitat conservation and research about the wild panda population.

In 1980 the World Wildlife Fund (WWF), a conservation organization, began to work with China to help save the giant panda from extinction. With WWF help, the Chinese government has made many more nature reserves and new ones are planned. The research centers carry out research to attempt to answer questions (such as how much space the panda needs to survive) and to solve problems (such as enforcing laws to protect them and their bamboo habitat).

Many people agree that it is up to China to save the giant panda with funds, support, and more research help from the rest of the world.

We all hope, like Ming Chi, that the giant panda can remain, for generations to come, China's national treasure.

For more information about zoo pandas and panda facts on the Internet:

San Diego Zoo: http://www.sandiegozoo.org/special/pandas/panda__baby__facts.html
ZooAtlanta: http://www.zooatlanta.org
WWF: www.worldwildlife.org

Glossary

bamboo (bam-BOO) a kind of woody grass that can grow 10 to 12 feet high. There are many kinds of bamboo, and pandas eat different parts of it in different seasons. They eat the stems, leaves, branches, and young shoots.

bei-shung (bei-SHUNG) in Chinese, *bei-shung* means "white bear" or "panda."

Chinese language the Chinese language has no alphabet. The writing is made up of drawings called characters. The common spoken language (as used in this book) is *putongua* (pu-TON-gu-a), or Mandarin (MAN-dar-in).

enclosure (en-CLO-sure) in natural habitat enclosures, pandas can roam freely. Male and female pandas are sometimes put together in the hope that they will mate and produce young.

predator (PRED-a-tor) an animal that hunts prey to survive. Adult pandas have few predator enemies, but the sick and the young may be preyed upon by leopards, martens, golden cats, wild dogs, and brown bears.

provinces (PROV-in-ces) China is divided into areas called provinces. Today, pandas are found only in the provinces of Sichuan, Gansu, and Shaanxi.

red panda the endangered red panda of China weighs only about 12 pounds. It is rust red with a foxlike face and a ringed tail like a raccoon's. It eats mostly bamboo, but includes more foods in its diet than the giant panda.

reserve (re-SERVE) land that is set aside to protect habitats and wild animals. In China several reserves provide protection for the panda.

tranquilizer (TRAN-quil-i-zer) a drug that is used to make humans or animals calm. The right dose must be given to be sure they later awaken safely.

Welcome to the Young Readers' series!

These learning stories have been created to introduce young children to the study of animals.

Children's earliest exposure to reading is usually through fiction. Stories read aloud invite children into the world of words and imagination. If children are read to frequently, this becomes a highly anticipated form of entertainment. Often that same pleasure is felt when children learn to read on their own. Nonfiction books are also read aloud to children but generally when they are older. However, interest in the "real" world emerges early in life, as soon as children develop a sense of wonder about everything around them.

There are a number of excellent read-aloud natural-science books available. Educators and parents agree that children love nonfiction books about animals. Unfortunately, there are very few that can be read *by* young children. One of the goals of the Young Readers' series is to happily fill that gap!

The Giant Panda is one in a series of learning stories designed to appeal to young readers. In the classroom, the series can be incorporated into literature-based or whole-language programs, and would be especially suitable for science theme teaching units. Within planned units, each book may serve as a springboard to immersion techniques that include hands-on activities, field study trips, and additional research and reading. Many of the books are also concerned with the threatened or endangered status of the species studied and the role even young people can play in the preservation plan.

These books can also serve as read-aloud for young children. Weaving information through a story form lends itself easily to reading aloud. Hopefully, this book and others in the series will provide entertainment and wonder for both young readers and listeners.

C. A.